Let's Fly

FLYING CARS

by Wendy Hinote Lanier

FOCUS READERS

www.focusreaders.com

Focus Readers is distributed by North Star Editions:
sales@northstareditions.com | 888-417-0195

Produced for Focus Readers by Red Line Editorial.

Photographs ©: Uli Deck/picture-alliance/dpa/AP Images, cover, 1; WENN Ltd/Alamy, 4–5; Agnieszka Skalska/Shutterstock Images, 7; Courtesy of the San Diego Air & Space Museum, 8–9; Ed Bailey/AP Images, 11; Hartmut Reeh/picture-alliance/dpa/AP Images, 13; Agia/Shutterstock Images, 14–15; Valery Hache/AFP/Getty Images, 17; Claude Paris/AP Images, 19, 24; Mmassel/iStockphoto, 20–21, 26–27, 29; Julian Stratenschulte/dpa/Alamy, 22

Library of Congress Cataloging-in-Publication Data
Names: Lanier, Wendy Hinote, author.
Title: Flying cars / by Wendy Hinote Lanier.
Description: Lake Elmo, MN : Focus Readers, [2019] | Series: Let's fly | Audience: Grades 4 to 6. | Includes bibliographical references and index.
Identifiers: LCCN 2018030375 (print) | LCCN 2018031676 (ebook) | ISBN 9781641855129 (PDF) | ISBN 9781641854542 (ebook) | ISBN 9781641853385 (hardcover) | ISBN 9781641853965 (pbk.)
Subjects: LCSH: Flying automobiles--Juvenile literature.
Classification: LCC TL684.8 (ebook) | LCC TL684.8 .L36 2019 (print) | DDC 629.04/6--dc23
LC record available at https://lccn.loc.gov/2018030375

Printed in the United States of America
Mankato, MN
October, 2018

About the Author

Wendy Hinote Lanier is a native Texan and former elementary teacher who writes and speaks for children and adults on a variety of topics. She is the author of more than 30 books for children and young adults.

TABLE OF CONTENTS

CHAPTER 1

Test Flight 5

CHAPTER 2

Early Flying Cars 9

CHAPTER 3

Part Car, Part Plane 15

CHAPTER 4

Flying Cars Today 21

HOW IT WORKS

Folding Pieces 26

Focus on Flying Cars • 28

Glossary • 30

To Learn More • 31

Index • 32

CHAPTER 1

TEST FLIGHT

It is a clear spring day in the Netherlands. **Engineers** wait at the edge of a runway. Soon a vehicle approaches. It looks similar to a car. But it has only three wheels.

This illustration shows one company's flying car design.

The car stops. The driver gets out. He unfolds a **rotor** on the roof. Now the car looks like a helicopter. It zooms back down the runway. Soon it is in the air.

The test is a success. But the engineers have more work to do. Six years later, the car is ready.

FUN FACT

The Geneva International Motor Show is held in Switzerland. More than 650,000 people attend each year.

Flying cars at the Geneva International Motor Show can have many different shapes.

It is part of the Geneva International Motor Show. This event shows off the latest car technology.

CHAPTER 2

EARLY FLYING CARS

The first flying car was built in 1917. It was called the Autoplane. However, it barely got off the ground. Other early flying cars faced problems as well. One car, the Arrowbile, had three wheels.

The Arrowbile was a flying car with long, slanted wings.

Its wings were slanted back. In the air, it used a **propeller**. The Arrowbile made a test flight in 1937. But only five were ever built.

Later, an inventor **adapted** an airplane for the road. He called it

CHANGING SHAPE

The Airphibian could fly 120 miles per hour (193 km/h). Its wings and tail could be removed when it drove on the ground. So could its propeller. These parts could be stored inside the car's body. The car could go 50 miles per hour (80 km/h) on the road.

Robert Edison Fulton Jr. (right) invented the Airphibian in the 1940s.

the Airphibian. The US government approved it in 1950. But the inventor could not find a company that would pay to build it.

The US government approved a new design in 1966. The Aerocar had four wheels. Its wings could fold back. The wings were pulled behind the car as it drove on the ground.

On land, the Aerocar reached speeds of 60 miles per hour (97 km/h). It could go 110 miles

FUN FACT

In the movie *Planes*, the character Franz is based on the Aerocar.

An Aerocar takes off from a runway.

per hour (177 km/h) in the air. But plans to produce this car had to be canceled. Once again, the company did not have enough money.

AIRBUS
ŠKODA
POP.UP
NEXT

CHAPTER 3

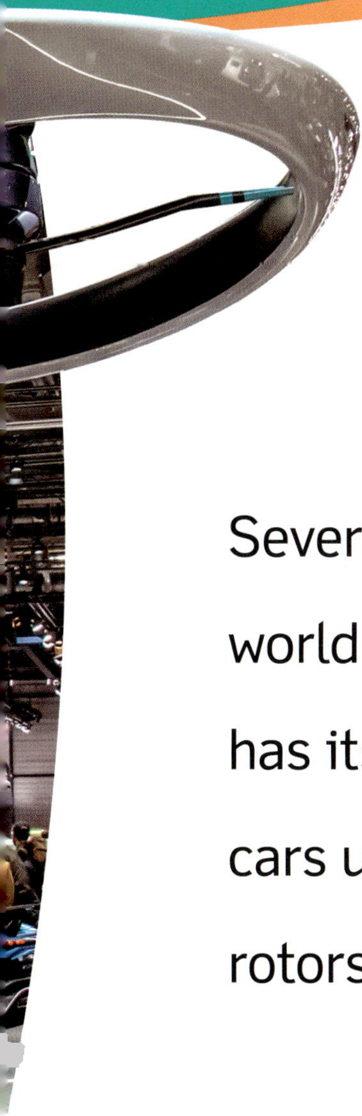

PART CAR, PART PLANE

Several companies around the world make flying cars. Each one has its own design. Some flying cars use propellers. Others have rotors. Still others use ducted fans.

One flying car design by Airbus (top) uses four ducted fans.

Ducted fans are propellers inside a ring or tube.

Some flying cars have gasoline engines. Other cars use electric motors. Many use a mix of both. The engines or motors provide power. They spin the car's propellers or rotors. The spinning blades help

FUN FACT

Some flying car designs do not need a pilot. They use computers to fly automatically.

the car go up into the air. The car's wings also help provide **lift**.

Designers must follow strict safety rules. Some requirements are for cars. Others are for planes.

Every car needs to have safety belts. It must have a **cage**. And it must have **crumple zones**. These parts protect passengers in a crash. Airplanes must follow another set of

SAFETY IN THE AIR

The first airplane flight took place in 1903. At first, there were no rules for flying. Accidents were common. In 1926, the United States passed laws about flying to keep people safe. Later, the Federal Aviation Agency (FAA) was created. The FAA makes rules for flying in the United States. Other countries have rules for airplanes, too.

In a flying car, passengers sit inside a compartment that protects them.

rules. These rules limit things such as weight and wing shape.

EXPERIMENTAL

CHAPTER 4

FLYING CARS TODAY

Most flying cars are still in their early stages. Companies continue to improve their designs. Some cars need a runway to take off or land. Other cars can take off vertically like a helicopter does.

A Terrafugia lands on a runway after a test flight in 2013.

A man tests a three-wheeled flying car in Germany.

For example, the PAL-V Liberty is made in the Netherlands. This car needs a runway to take off. But it can land like a helicopter.

Many designs have wings that can fold. One is the Terrafugia TF-X. This car is made in the United States. Its wings and rotors fold away when it drives on the ground.

The AeroMobil also has folding wings. This car is made in Slovakia. In the air, it is powered by gasoline.

FUN FACT

The PAL-V Liberty can speed through the air at 112 miles per hour (180 km/h). On the ground, it can go 100 miles per hour (161 km/h).

The AeroMobil's wings can unfold in less than three minutes.

On the ground, the car gets power from electricity.

Some flying cars cannot go on roads. These cars can only travel through the air. The German Lilium Eagle is one example. The Eagle gets power from **jet engines**. It takes off and lands like a helicopter. It has two seats for passengers.

SIMPLER SHAPES

Following rules for both cars and airplanes can be difficult. So, some designers make vehicles that only fly. These vehicles have to follow only one set of rules. Other designers make their vehicles more like motorcycles. Safety rules for motorcycles are easier to follow than rules for cars.

HOW IT WORKS

FOLDING PIECES

The Terrafugia TF-X has two wings. Each wing has an electric motor at the end. The motors attach to rotors. When the rotors spin, the car takes off vertically. Once the car is in the air, the rotors tilt forward and fold back. After that, a ducted fan near the back of the car provides **thrust**.

On the ground, the wings fold near the car's sides. The TF-X can drive on roads like a regular car. It can even park in a garage. When the car's motors need to be recharged, the driver plugs the car into a charging station.

A Terrafugia folds its wings after landing.

FOCUS ON

FLYING CARS

Write your answers on a separate piece of paper.

1. Write a sentence describing one of the early flying car designs.
2. Which flying car would you most like to own? Why would you choose that one?
3. When was the first flying car invented?
   - A. 1903
   - B. 1917
   - C. 1966
4. What would happen if a flying car's rotors broke?
   - A. The car could not take off vertically.
   - B. The car could not turn on.
   - C. The car could not drive on the ground.

5. What does **requirements** mean in this book?

Designers must follow strict safety rules. Some ***requirements*** *are for cars.*

A. things that make cars go faster
B. things people do not have to follow
C. things people are told or expected to do

6. What does **canceled** mean in this book?

But plans to produce this car had to be ***canceled****. Once again, the company did not have enough money.*

A. stopped
B. done faster
C. kept the same

Answer key on page 32.

GLOSSARY

adapted
Changed to better function in a certain place or situation.

cage
A strong part of a vehicle's frame that surrounds the passengers.

crumple zones
Parts of a car that crunch up to help absorb the force of a crash.

engineers
People who design and create buildings or machines.

jet engines
Engines that produce power by burning a mixture of fuel and air and sending out a stream of hot gases.

lift
An upward force that causes a vehicle to rise into the air.

propeller
A vertical set of spinning blades that provide thrust, which moves a vehicle forward like an airplane.

rotor
A horizontal set of spinning blades that provide lift, which moves a vehicle up into the air like a helicopter.

thrust
A force that pushes air backward and causes a vehicle to move forward.

TO LEARN MORE

BOOKS

Glass, Andrew. *Flying Cars: The True Story*. Boston: Clarion Books, 2015.

Petersen, Christine. *Inventing the Hybrid Car*. Mankato, MN: The Child's World, 2016.

Zuchora-Walske, Christine. *Self-Driving Cars*. Minneapolis: Abdo Publishing, 2018.

NOTE TO EDUCATORS

Visit **www.focusreaders.com** to find lesson plans, activities, links, and other resources related to this title.

INDEX

A

Aerocar, 12–13
AeroMobil, 23–24
Airphibian, 10–11
Arrowbile, 9–10
Autoplane, 9

D

ducted fans, 15–16, 26

E

engines, 16, 25

G

Geneva International Motor Show, 6–7

H

helicopter, 6, 21–22, 25

L

Lilium Eagle, 25

M

motorcycles, 25
motors, 16, 26

P

PAL-V, 22–23
propeller, 10, 15–17

R

rotors, 6, 15–16, 23, 26
runway, 5–6, 21–22

S

safety rules, 17–19, 25

T

Terrafugia, 23, 26

W

wheels, 5, 9, 12, 17
wings, 10, 12, 17, 19, 23, 26

Answer Key: 1. Answers will vary; **2.** Answers will vary; **3.** B; **4.** A; **5.** C; **6.** A